THE SEVENTIES
part four

Ain't No Sunshine, 2
Always And Forever, 6
Baby, I Love Your Way, 12
Big Yellow Taxi, 22
Boogie Wonderland, 26
Breakaway, 17
Breakfast In America, 34
Dancing Queen, 42
December 1963 (Oh What A Night), 38
Give A Little Bit, 52
Harvest For The World, 47
The Hustle, 56
I'll Never Love This Way Again, 60
If You Don't Know Me By Now, 66
It's Too Late, 63
Just My Imagination (Running Away With Me), 70
Lady Marmalade, 74
Le Freak, 81
Light My Fire, 78
Livin' Thing, 84
Lost In Music, 88
Love Don't Live Here Anymore, 91
Lovely Day, 97
Maggie May, 94
Me And Mrs Jones, 100
My Coo Ca Choo, 104
One Day In Your Life, 108
Rock With You, 115
Since You've Been Gone, 112
So Far Away, 118
Sometimes When We Touch, 122
A Song For You, 126
Street Life, 132
Take It To The Limit, 136
Through The Eyes Of Love (Theme From "Ice Castles"), 140
Top Of The World, 146
We've Only Just Begun, 143
Wishing On A Star, 150
You Make Me Feel Brand New, 158
You're The First, The Last, My Everything, 154

Production: Sadie Cook
Music processed by Global Music Solutions, Surrey SM6 9BT
Cover design by Headline Publicity Limited

Published 1997

© International Music Publications Limited
Southend Road, Woodford Green, Essex IG8 8HN, England

AIN'T NO SUNSHINE

Words and Music by BILL WITHERS

ALWAYS AND FOREVER

Words and Music by ROD TEMPERTON

Ooh!

Oh!_____

Al - ways and for - ev - er,_____ each mo - ment with__ you_____
There'll al - ways be sun - shine_____ when I look at__ you._____

BABY, I LOVE YOUR WAY

Words and Music by PETER FRAMPTON

Reggae

Ooh, ba-by I love your way ev-ery day, yeah.

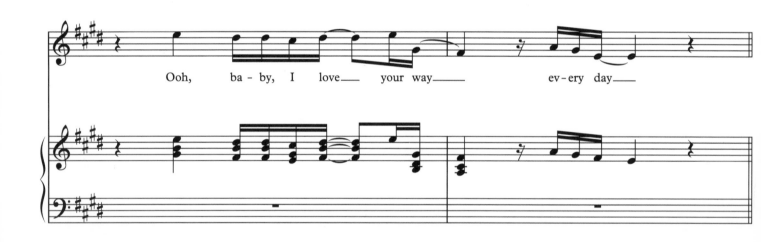

Ooh, ba-by, I love your way ev-ery day

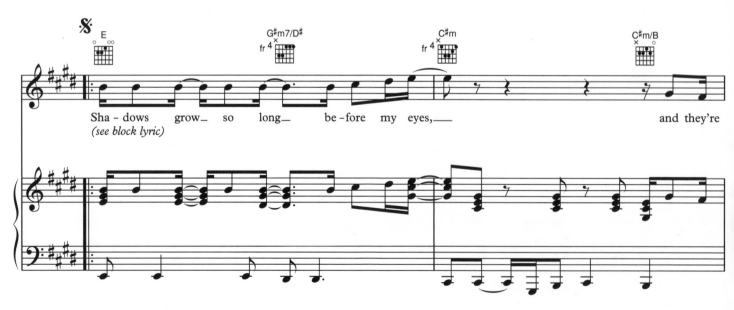

Sha-dows grow so long be-fore my eyes, and they're
(see block lyric)

I wan-na tell you I love___ your way___ ev- ery day.___

I wan-na be with you night___ and day.___ The

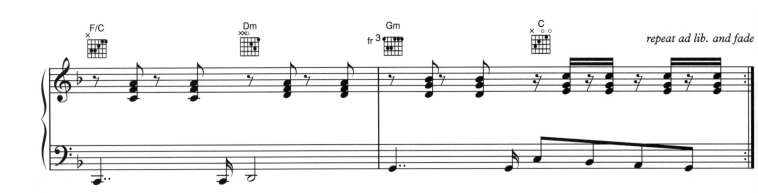

Verse 2:
The moon appears to shine and light the sky
With the help of some fireflies
I wonder how they have the power to shine;
I can see them under the pine

Verse 3: (Instrumental)

Verse 4:
I can see the sunset in your eyes
Brown and gray and blue besides
Clouds are stalking islands in the sun
I wish I could buy one out of season

BREAKAWAY

Words and Music by BENNY GALLAGHER and GRAHAM LYLE

Time has_ come for you to wak-en in an-oth-er coun-try, greet the morn-ing un-der for-eign skies,_ leav-ing me to face a-no-ther Mon-day. It's not ea-sy to get__ by.

BIG YELLOW TAXI

Words and Music by JONI MITCHELL

Verse 3:
Hey farmer, farmer, put away your DDT now
Give me spots on my apples
But leave me with the birds and the bees, please

Verse 4: (Instrumental)

Verse 5:
Late last night I heard the screen door slam
And a big yellow taxi carried off my old man

BOOGIE WONDERLAND

Words and Music by ALLEE WILLIS and JON LIND

BREAKFAST IN AMERICA

Words and Music by RICK DAVIES and ROGER HODGSON

Take a look at my___ girl - friend; she's the on - ly one I got.
Could we have kip - pers for___ break - fast, mum-my dear, mum-my dear?

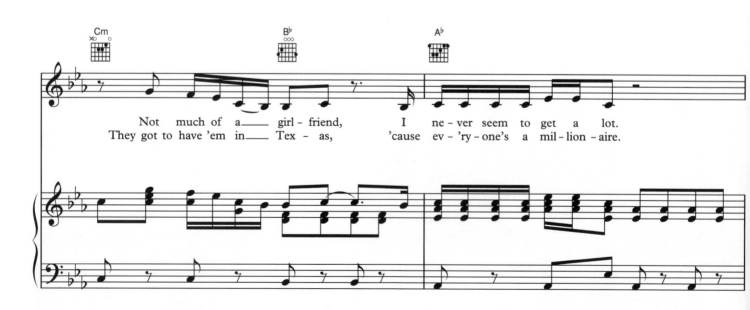

Not much of a___ girl - friend, I ne - ver seem to get a lot.
They got to have 'em in___ Tex - as, 'cause ev - 'ry-one's a mil-lion-aire.

oh,_____ hey_ oh._____ hey_ oh,_ hey_ oh,_____ hey_ oh,_____ hey_ oh._ Na na

na, na na na na na_____ na._____

Verse 3:
Don't you look at my girlfriend
She's the only one I got
Not much of a girlfriend
I never seem to get a lot

Take a jumbo 'cross the water
Like to see America
See the girls in California
I'm hoping it's going to come true
But there's not a lot I can do

DECEMBER 1963 (OH WHAT A NIGHT)

Words and Music by BOB GAUDIO and JUDY PARKER

DANCING QUEEN

Words and Music by BENNY ANDERSSON, STIG ANDERSON
and BJÖRN ULVAEUS

A - ny - bo - dy could be that guy___
You're a tea - ser you turn 'em on___

night is young and the mu - sic's high.
leave 'em burn - ing and then you're gone

With a bit___ of rock mu - sic
look - ing out___ for an - oth - er

ev - 'ry - thing___ is fine___
a - ny - one___ will do___

you're in the mood for a dance___

and when___ you get the___ chance,_____ you are___ the

danc - ing— queen.

1.

Dig in the

2.

dancing— queen._____

repeat and fade

Dig in the

HARVEST FOR THE WORLD

Words and Music by O'KELLY ISLEY, MARVIN ISLEY, RONALD ISLEY
RUDOLPH ISLEY, ERNIE ISLEY and CHRIS JASPER

A har-vest for— the world.— A

Verse 2:

A nation planted, so concerned with gain
As the seasons come and go, greater grows the pain
And far too many are feeling the strain
Oh, when will there be a harvest for the world?

Verse 3:

Dress me up for battle when all I want is peace
Those of us who pay the price come home with the least
And nation after nation are turning into peace
Oh, when will there be a harvest for the world?

GIVE A LITTLE BIT

Words and Music by RICK DAVIES and ROGER HODGSON

Moderately

Give a lit-tle bit,_____ give a lit-tle bit__ of your love__ to me.

I'll give a lit-tle bit,_____ I'll give a lit-tle bit__ of my love

I'll give a lit-tle bit__ of my love

THE HUSTLE

By VAN McCOY

Do the hus - tle!

I'LL NEVER LOVE THIS WAY AGAIN

Words by WILL JENNINGS
Music by RICHARD KERR

IT'S TOO LATE

Words and Music by CAROLE KING and TONI STERN

Stayed in bed all morn-in' just to pass the time.___ There's some-thing wrong here, there can
used to be so ea-sy liv-ing here with you;___ you were light and breez-y and I
There'll be good times a-gain for me and you;___ but we just can't stay to-ge-ther.

be no de-ny-in'. One of us___ is chang-in' or may-be we've just___ stopped try-
knew just what to do. Now you look so___ un-hap-py and I feel___ like___ a___ fool.
Don't you feel it, too? Still I'm glad___ for what we had and how I___ once___ loved___ you.

IF YOU DON'T NOW ME BY KNOW

Words and Music by LEON HUFF and KENNETH GAMBLE

Slow 3

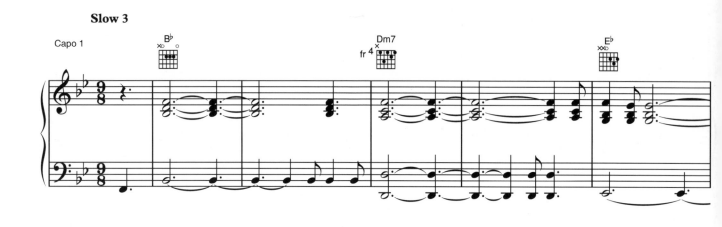

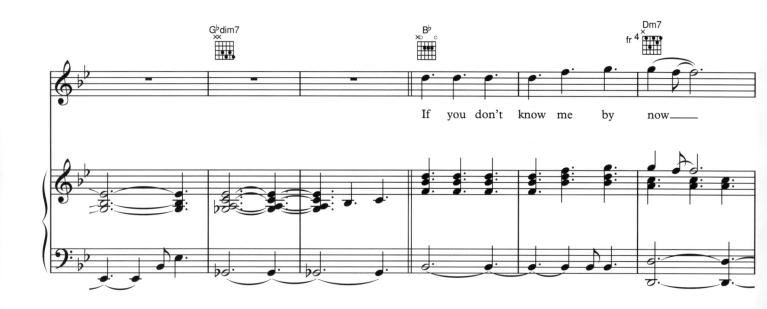

If you don't know me by now____

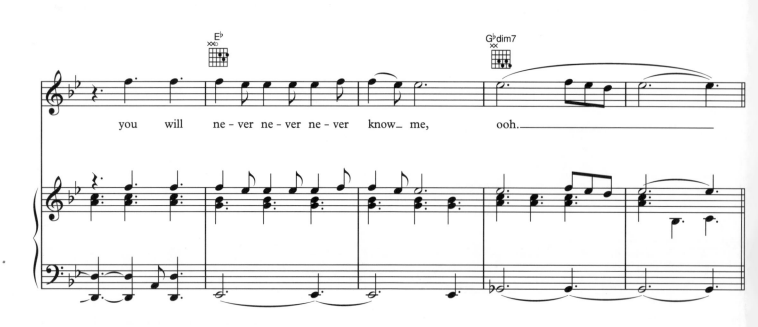

you will ne-ver ne-ver ne-ver know__ me, ooh._____

JUST MY IMAGINATION
(RUNNING AWAY WITH ME)

Words and Music by NORMAN WHITFIELD and BARRETT STRONG

LADY MARMALADE

Words and Music by BOB CREWE and KENNY NOLAN

LIGHT MY FIRE

Words and Music by THE DOORS

LE FREAK

Words and Music by NILE RODGERS and BERNARD EDWARDS

do-in' it night and day.—

to the Fif-ty- four.—

Al-low us, we'll show you the way.

Find a spot out on the floor.

Freak

out!

Le Freak, c'est chic. Freak out!

Freak out! Le

Freak, c'est chic. Freak out!

Freak

LIVIN' THING

Words and Music by JEFF LYNNE

Freely

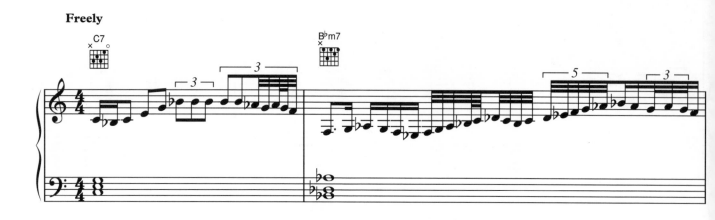

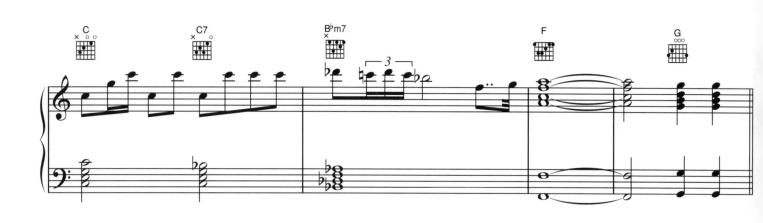

a tempo (with a beat)

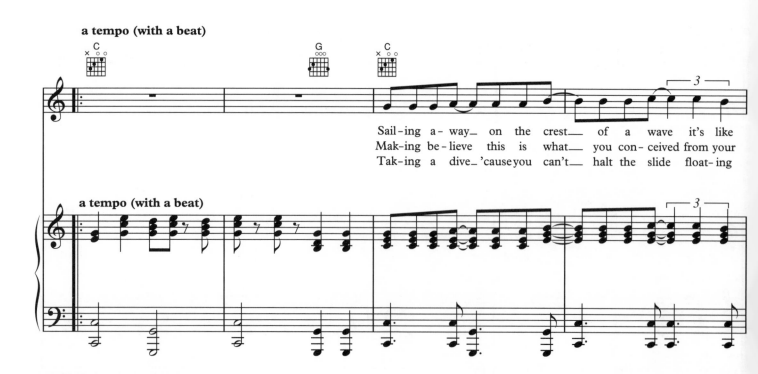

Sail-ing a-way___ on the crest___ of a wave it's like
Mak-ing be-lieve this is what___ you con-ceived from your
Tak-ing a dive___ 'cause you can't___ halt the slide float-ing

LOST IN MUSIC

Words and Music by NILE RODGERS and BERNARD EDWARDS

LOVE DON'T LIVE HERE ANYMORE

Words and Music by MILE GREGORY

(1.) lived in - side_ of_ me, there was no - thing I_____ could con -ceed that you would-n't
(2.) live here a - ny_ more, just emp - ti - ness and mem - o - ries of
(3.) wind - mills of_ my_ eyes, ev - ery - one_____ can see the

do for me. Trou - ble seems
what we had be - fore. You
lone - li - ness in - side me. Why d'you have to

— so far a - way,_ you changed it right a - way,_ ba - by.
went a - way, found an - oth - er place to stay, an - oth - er_ home.
go a - way? Don't you know I miss you so? I need_ your_ love.

MAGGIE MAY

Words and Music by ROD STEWART and MARTIN QUITTENTON

Wake up, Mag - gie, I think I got some-thing to say to you.— It's

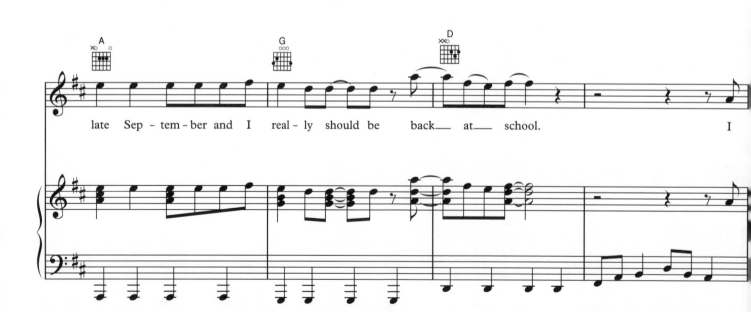

late Sep-tem-ber and I real-ly should be back— at— school. I

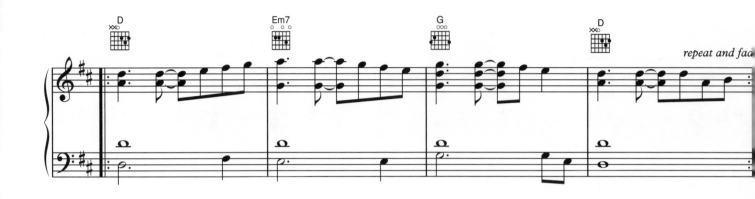

repeat and fad

Verse 2:
The morning sun, when it's in your face
Really shows your age
But that don't worry me none
In my eyes, you're everything
I laughed at all your jokes
My love you didn't need to coax
Oh, Maggie, I couldn't have tried any more
You led me away from home
Just to save you from being alone
You stole my soul, and that's a pain I can do without

Verse 3:
All I needed was a friend
To lend a guiding hand
But you turned into a lover and, mother, what a lover!
You wore me out
All you did was wreck my bed
And, in the morning, kick me in the head
Oh, Maggie, I couldn't have tried any more
You led me away from home
'Cause you didn't want to be alone
You stole my heart. I couldn't leave you if I tried

Verse 4:
I suppose I could collect my books
And get on back to school
Or steal my daddy's cue
And make a living out of playing pool
Or find myself a rock 'n' roll band
That needs a helping hand
Oh, Maggie, I wish I'd never seen your face
You made a first-class fool out of me
But I'm as blind as a fool can be
You stole my heart, but I love you anyway

LOVELY DAY

Words and Music by SKIP SCARBOROUGH and BILL WITHERS

ME AND MRS JONES

Words and Music by LEON HUFF, KENNETH GAMBLE
and CARY GILBERT

102

MY COO CA CHOO

Words and Music by PETER SHELLEY

Moderately

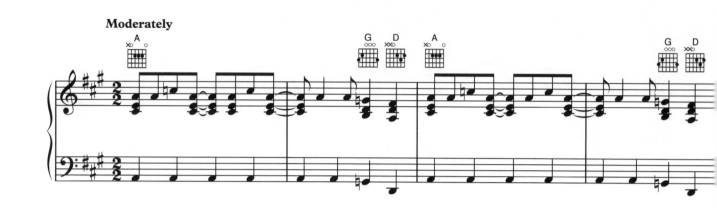

Yeah!

Coo!   Coo!   I   just   want   you.   I   real - ly   love   the
Tom   cat!   You   know   where   it's   at.   Come   on,   let's
Night   time's   a   lone - ly   time.   When   you're   gone,   I'm

106

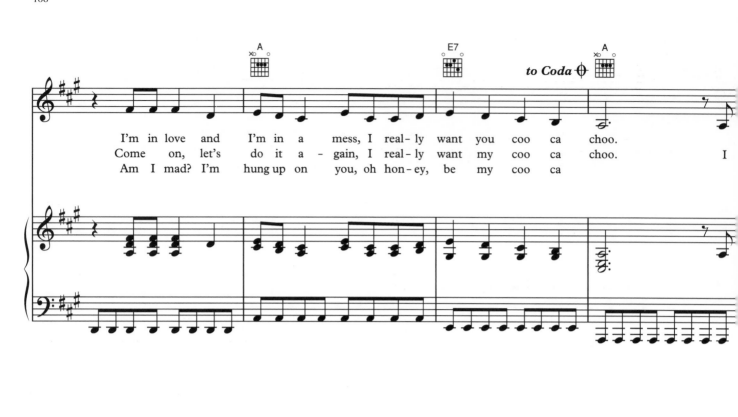

I'm in love and I'm in a mess, I real-ly want you coo ca choo.
Come on, let's do it a - gain, I real-ly want my coo ca choo.
Am I mad? I'm hung up on you, oh hon-ey, be my coo ca

to Coda

I

love you, yes, I love ya, yes, I, I love my coo ca choo.
Want you, yes, I want ya, yes, I, I real-ly do want

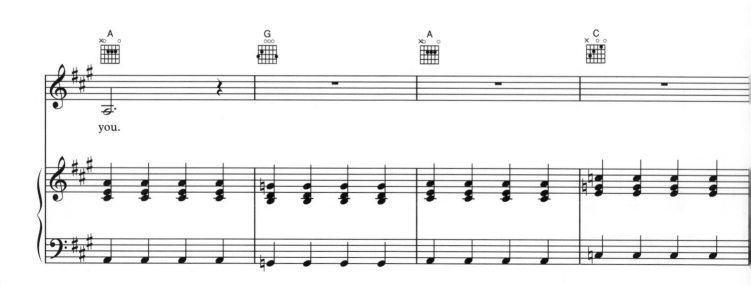

you.

ONE DAY IN YOUR LIFE

Words by RENEE ARMAND
Music by SAMUEL F BROWN III

and I'll____ be there.

SINCE YOU'VE BEEN GONE

Words and Music by RUSS BALLARD

ROCK WITH YOU

Words and Music by ROD TEMPERTON

SO FAR AWAY

Words and Music by CAROLE KING

So far a-way! Does-n't a-ny-bo-dy stay in one place_ a-ny_ more?

It would be so fine to see_ your face at my door. Does-n't help_ to know you're just

SOMETIMES WHEN WE TOUCH

Words by DAN HILL
Music by BARRY MANN

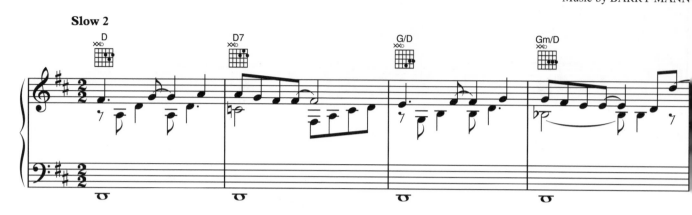

A SONG FOR YOU

Words and Music by LEON RUSSELL

words don't come to-geth-er,____ lis-ten to the me-lo-dy, 'cause my love's____ in there hid-ing.

I love you in a place where there's no space or time. I love you for my life 'cause you're a

friend of mine. And when my life is ov - er, re-mem-ber when we were to-ge - ther.

STREET LIFE

Words by WILL JENNINGS
Music by JOE SAMPLE

TAKE IT TO THE LIMIT

Words and Music by DON HENLEY, GLENN FREY
and RANDY MEISNER

THROUGH THE EYES OF LOVE
(THEME FROM 'ICE CASTLES')

Words by CAROLE BAYER-SAGER
Music by MARVIN HAMLISCH

Please, don't let this feel-ing end, it's ev-ery-thing I am, ev-ery-thing I

now_____ I can take the time, I can see my life as it comes up

Please, don't let this feel-ing end, it might not come a-gain, and I want to re-

WE'VE ONLY JUST BEGUN

Words by PAUL WILLIAMS
Music by ROGER NICHOLS

We've on-ly just be-gun to live, white lace and
Be-fore the ris-ing sun we fly, so ma-ny
And when the even-ing comes we smile. So much of

pro-mi-ses, a kiss for luck and we're on our way.
roads to choose, we start out walk-ing and learn to run.
life a-head, we'll find a place where there's room to grow.

working to-geth-er day to day, to- geth- er.___

D.%. al Coda

CODA

And yes, we've just be - gun.___

TOP OF THE WORLD

Words by JOHN BETTIS
Music by RICHARD CARPENTER

Such a feel-ing's com-ing ov-er me._____ There is
Some-thing in___ the wind has learned my name_____ and it's

WISHING ON A STAR

Words and Music by BILLIE CALVIN

153

YOU'RE THE FIRST, THE LAST, MY EVERYTHING

Words and Music by BARRY WHITE, TONY SEPE
and STERLING RADCLIFFE

Moderately

(Spoken) *We got it together, didn't we . . . nobody but you and me . . .*
we've got it together, babe . . .

The first, my___ last, my___ eve-ry-thing   and the

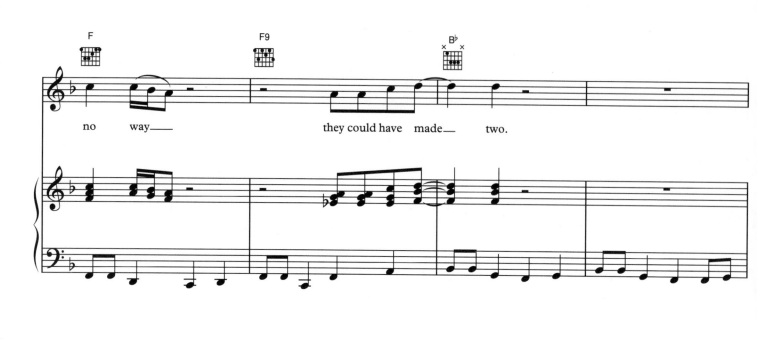

no way___ they could have made___ two.

You're, you're all I'm liv-ing for.___ Your love I'll keep for-ev - er more. You're

1.

___ the first, you're___ the last, my ev - ery thing.

157

— the first,

the last,— my ev-er-y-thing.

Verse 2:
In you I find so many things
A love so new only you could bring
Can't you see if you . . . you make me feel this way
You're like a fresh morning dew
Or a brand new day
I see so many ways that I
Can love you 'til the day I die
You're my reality
Yet I'm lost in a dream
You're the first, the last, my everything

YOU MAKE ME FEEL BRAND NEW

Words and Music by THOMAS BELL and LINDA CREED

My love,

I'll nev-er find the words, my love,_____ to tell you how I feel, my
when-ev-er I was in-sec-ure,_____ you built me up and made me

love. Mere words_____ could not_____ ex-plain_____ Prec - ious
sure. You gave_____ my pride_____ back to me._____ Prec - ious

160